D E D I C A T I O N

As our century races toward its conclusion, much has changed since the first publication of this book and the national tour of the quilts it contains. There has been an ever-broadening acceptance of the quilt as important folk art by institutions, museums and galleries, but perhaps more importantly, a deeper understanding and appreciation by the American people of quilts and their makers as a valuable unwritten history of women's lives.

Due largely to the many regional quilt "searches" and individual and group research projects and publications, much of the folklore of misinformation has been erased and replaced by facts that surprisingly do nothing to diminish the romantic and sentimental attachments we hold to these labors of love and usefulness.

The death of my father, Edwin Binney, 3rd, in 1986 has left a deep personal void, and one in the collecting world as well. It was his wish, as it is mine, that the quilts we so joyously collected together live on to the enjoyment of the American people, and to this end, a significant number of quilts from our collection were gifted, and will continue to be gifted, to the New England Quilt Museum of Lowell, Massachusetts, for its permanent collection.

I wish to rededicate this book in loving memory of my father, Edwin Binney, 3rd, my late husband, Sidney Winslow, and Michael Kile, who all made the original possible.

A special thank-you to Roderick Kiracofe, friend and one of the original "godfathers" of this project, who believed this work was worth republishing, and to Larry Stone of Rutledge Hill Press for making it possible to do so.

> Gail Binney (Winslow) Stiles
> Ebensburg, Pennsylvania 1993

*I*t is with great pleasure that SITES once again presents to the public an exhibition from the rich and varied collections of Edwin Binney, 3rd.

Over SITES' thirty-two years of programming, it has been our good fortune to have collaborated with Dr. Binney on four previous exhibitions, ranging in subject matter from Islamic art to the lithographs and engravings of the French master Eugène Delacroix. Dr. Binney's wide-ranging interests and scholarship have provided international audiences unique opportunities to view these private collections and to appreciate their interpretation through programming and publications.

We are grateful to Dr. Binney and to his daughter, Gail Binney-Winslow, for the loan of this significant selection of American quilts from their collection of more than one hundred. The forty-five pieces chosen for tour cover two hundred years and offer an in-depth view of the design creativity and artistic craftsmanship that are the hallmarks of fine American quiltmaking.

To realize this project, SITES worked co-operatively with our colleagues at the San Diego Museum of Art. We acknowledge and thank them for their contribution to the organization of this exhibition. At SITES, Eileen Rose served as exhibition co-ordinator for this project, deftly handling administrative concerns and supervising all aspects of this exhibition's international tour.

We at SITES are delighted to renew our association with Dr. Binney and to welcome the contribution of quiltmaker/collector Gail Binney-Winslow on this very American exhibition, HOMAGE TO AMANDA.

Peggy A. Loar
Director
Smithsonian Institution Traveling
Exhibition Service (SITES)

HOMAGE TO AMANDA

H O M A G E

to

Amanda

Two Hundred Years of American Quilts

FROM THE COLLECTION OF EDWIN BINNEY, 3RD & GAIL BINNEY-WINSLOW

RUTLEDGE HILL PRESS
NASHVILLE, TENNESSEE

Published in Nashville, Tennessee, by Rutledge Hill Press, 211 Seventh
Avenue North, Nashville, Tennessee 37219

Originally published by Roderick Kiracofe/RK Press, San Francisco,
California.

Library of Congress Cataloging-in-Publication Data

Binney. Edwin,
    Homage to Amanda : two hundred years of American quilts / from the collection of
Edwin Binney, 3rd & Gail Binney-Winslow.
        p.   cm.
    Includes bibliographical references.
    ISBN 1-55853-269-2 — ISBN 1-55853-268-4 (pbk.)
    1. Quilts—United States—History.   I. Binney-Winslow, Gail.
II. Title.
NK9112.B52 1993   93-37663
746.9'7'0973—dc20   CIP

    1 2 3 4 5 6 7 8 — 99 98 97 96 95 94 93
Printed in Hong Kong through Palace Press

Edwin Binney, 3rd and the San Diego Museum of Art have had a long and rewarding association. A Trustee of this Museum since 1976, and its friend and patron for more than a decade previously, Dr. Binney has enriched that friendship for us all with his careful scholarship, his encouragement of excellence and his lively wit. It has been our pleasure to host several other exhibitions of Dr. Binney's varied and important collections. Among these have been Islamic miniature paintings of the Persian, Mughal and Deccani Schools, French paintings and graphics of the Romantic period and his comprehensive collection of the arts of the Ottoman Turkish Empire.

Now, we are honored and pleased to have been chosen to organize and present the current exhibition of American quilts, *Homage to Amanda,* drawn from the very personal collection of Dr. Binney and Gail Binney-Winslow and, under the auspices of the Smithsonian Institution Traveling Exhibition Service, to be able to share this most American subject with an international selection of museums.

Steven L. Brezzo
Director
San Diego Museum of Art

ACKNOWLEDGMENTS

*W*e wish to thank the following people for sharing their knowledge and providing helpful assistance in the preparation of this text:

Sonya Lee Barrington, San Francisco, California; Cuesta Benberry, St. Louis, Missouri; Barbara Brackman, Lawrence, Kansas; Patricia T. Herr, Lancaster, Pennsylvania; Lucy Hilty, Berkeley, California; Claire Lamers, Assistant Librarian, Long Island Historical Society, Brooklyn, New York; Edward Maeder, Curator of Costume, Los Angeles County Museum of Art, Los Angeles, California; Judy Mathieson, Woodland Hills, California; Penny McMorris, Bowling Green, Ohio; Patsy Orlofsky, South Salem, New York; Natalie Rothstein, Deputy Keeper, Department of Textiles and Dress, Victoria and Albert Museum, London, England; Julie Silber, Curator, Esprit Collection, San Francisco, California.

C O N T E N T S

Quiltmaking is an art form in which our appreciation of the work is often closely linked with our admiration for the maker, even when that maker is anonymous. Most good quilts have a special presence about them, expressive of the uncountable hours of attentive skill that they represent. It has been remarked by some conservative art historians that, if we fall to discussing the effort that went into a piece, then that piece is not "art," but rather "mere craft." This trivializing judgment, irritating though it can be for decorative arts specialists, does at least recognize an important aspect of quilting as an art form. Were "mere craft" the only impulse here, then quilters would save themselves the time, making nothing more complex than furniture blankets.

Naturally, intensive labor is not in itself enough to produce a fine quilt. Without an inspired sense of design, the quilter's efforts have been wasted. It is exciting then to consider that there are so many truly beautiful quilts. They are the material evidence of the high aesthetic levels possible in American vernacular design. Although American quilts were scorned in the nineteenth century by the educated spokesmen of "official" culture, later generations have come to recognize, and emulate, their graphic sophistication. It seems ironic, then, that many quilters of years past would say, "I wish I were creative," as they sat at their frames producing works of splendid creativity.

Perhaps it was this very confusion that freed nineteenth-century quilters from the stylistic restrictions of the "fine art" of their time. Instead they learned to please themselves, and to please other quilters. They played with color and shape, and evolved cryptic vocabularies of stitch and pattern, as satisfactory to themselves as were the fraternal rites of Masonic and Grange halls to their husbands. Other publications have already documented these social aspects of quilting. They have recorded the habits and thoughts of quilters, who, working singly or in groups, have in their quilting performed a ritual of continuity and nurture.

The ethnic and regional diversity of traditional American life was reflected in a similar diversity of American quilts. Technological and economic changes in the developing nation further encouraged this variety. The availability and cost of suitable fabrics, and rapid changes of fashion (especially in printed cottons), have exercised a continuous influence on quilt design in this country. One might say that this technical influence occurs most purely in quiltmaking, among all the traditional American folk-art media, despite the overriding factors of regional styles and the makers' personal choices.

Just as quilts reflect their makers' personalities and surroundings, so do quilt collections reveal their collectors. If a good quilt is the result of available materials, careful planning and months or years of patient work, so is a good quilt collection. In our own time, public interest in quilts shows as much diversity as do the quilts themselves. Some people are drawn to quilts as part of their family heritage, or from admiration for traditional ways of life. Others respond to the visual excitement of quilt patterns, or to the intricacies of fine stitching. Many contemporary quiltmakers seek antique quilts for inspiration, or for examples of successful solutions to technical problems.

Although most collectors confine themselves to a few of these factors, there are some who reach out to embrace the whole. This is the case with Edwin Binney, 3rd and Gail Binney-Winslow. Their partnership in assembling this collection embodies all of the aspects mentioned above, and others as well. Their approach to collecting is at once deeply personal and academically detached, a combination of two complex and creative personalities. Although most quilt exhibitions have focused solely on the quilts themselves and their makers, it has been our decision here to examine the personality of a single, private collection as well as the items in it. Collecting is, after all, a sustained creative act of itself, as much a part of art history as the forces that impelled the artists in the first place.

It has been my good fortune for the past several years to be able to observe the formation of the collection presented here. A chief pleasure throughout this time has been the many explorations and discussions of quilts with Ed and Gail, whose friendly and ever-passionate approach to the subject is so infectious.

William S. Chandler
Associate Curator of Decorative Art
San Diego Museum of Art

*I*t is virtually impossible for me to separate myself as quilter from my role as collector. It is, perhaps, this very two-sidedness that enhances each activity and expands my outlook, joy and sense of privilege in being involved with quilts. From these dual roles comes a deep and abiding respect for the quilt and the quiltmaker.

The recognition of the quilt as an art object is due largely to collections, galleries, museums and books focusing on its visual form and design, but the resurgence of national and world interest in quilts and quilting goes far beyond a simple visual impact, and evokes our need, as a people, to connect with our cultural and personal past.

Few objects, born of necessity and taking such a functional form, have been elevated to such artistic heights. This is not to say, however, that all quilts are "art objects" or were ever intended to be, as this collection might imply. The very survival of any of the early quilts shown here suggests the classification of "Best Quilts," so planned by their makers. We are fortunate that these quilts were protected, cherished and handed down through generations, but it must be kept in mind that these same quilters produced a staggering quantity of quilts destined and intended to be used up during their lifetimes.

The anonymity of most quiltmakers in the past leaves unanswered many questions regarding their personal histories and the provenance of their works. How and why were they motivated? Many gaps remain as to specific information about dating, design and the overall significance of the quilts themselves. No matter how much is written today on the aesthetic qualities, historical significance and technical merit of these quilts, the lack of information regarding the personal history of the quiltmaker will continue to foster romantic notions, "folklore" or exaggerations, in a vain attempt to fill in the gaps. How fortunate for future generations that the current period of quiltmaking will be better documented, both about the quilts themselves and about their creators.

In viewing this collection, we must bear in mind that there is little orderly linear progression in the development of quilting. As styles overlapped and new patterns were invented, it became obvious that quilters were as equally tied to traditions established in earlier periods as they were committed to establishing innovative designs and interpretations of their own. Quilters of both yesterday and today, influenced deeply by their own environment, have always taken what is familiar to them and added ingredients from their own imaginations and vision. Aided by technological developments and the availability of materials, they have fused this double influence into a pioneer spirit of melded tradition and the celebration of events and milestones in their own lives.

Quiltmaker and author Beth Gutcheon observes, in *The Quilt Design Workbook,* "American women have long had hearts and minds, but only a very few had voices." We submit these quilts as the voices of more than six generations of women. As labors of love, reflections of both simple pleasures and the deepest of emotions, they speak eloquently indeed.

None of us want this voice to dim or disappear, but as collectors and viewers with voracious appetites, we must exercise caution and restraint in the handling and exhibiting of all quilts. We need to increase our knowledge of good conservation and preservation methods. We need to encourage those trained in the documenting and housing of this special visual textile heritage. We can all take an active part by supporting local and regional efforts to identify, document and build permanent housing for already existing collections. In this way, the innovative, creative spirit which has produced this wonderful aspect of our total culture can continue to enrich our present emotional needs. We need secure and permanent homes for these endangered works of art.

Gail Binney-Winslow

Detail of no. 14.

*T*he father and daughter who have shared the joy of forming this collection and writing this text have almost nothing in common as collectors. The first step of the collection's formation was my inheritance of the candlewick spread (no. 1) signed and dated by Amanda Davisson, my great-great-grandmother (no. 1a). Yet this rare work would have remained a family heirloom only, had it not been for a fortuitous circumstance. My daughter, after many years of striving to find the proper artistic medium in which to create and produce, discovered needlework, and particularly quilting. The opening of her quilt shop, the former Nine Patch in San Diego, California, provided the second necessary step that has resulted in this collection. While she was dealing with antique quilts, I was truly seeing them for the first time. Hundreds of quilts suddenly became accessible for our appreciation and heightened understanding (and occasional distaste). While I learned that a quilt can be judged exactly as are other works of art, my daughter counted stitches, learned the technical nuances of the creative process and absorbed the craft of quilting. Together, we form an excellent team — never in agreement for the same reasons, but always able to discuss with and learn from one another. The result is this exhibition, which presents the status quo of our joint collecting efforts. The entire collection will undoubtedly be different by the time the present exhibition tour ends. For we are both bitten by the same bug — COLLECTING QUILTS!

A collection of any kind that is not obtained as an already-completed whole must grow and change in spurts. If there are gaps in the collection that must be filled, the mere availability of a needed example is frequently even more important than the presence or absence of the funds for its purchase. When the collectors' avowed aim is to assemble a representative group of fine examples that illustrate the entire field of that medium — complete in periods, styles, techniques and materials — the task becomes even more complex.

The present exhibition has been chosen from a group of American quilts that is almost three times as large. Our aim has been to include the finest examples, while avoiding duplication of types. Within the whole collection, my daughter and I have an avowed preference for indigo-blue-and-white quilts, and these have been selected for the show by very arbitrary criteria. This group of our personal favorites has been kept together as "Collectors'

Choice," the final section. We have done this to point up the visual appeal of these wonderful, elegant works. A fine collection, even when representative of an entire medium, should reflect, as much as possible, the motivation and personalities of its collectors.

The chronological points of division of the exhibition have been chosen arbitrarily. Yet, the groupings are valid, and the number of examples in each is very logical. Interestingly, any one of the four separate historical sections would make a good province for another quilt collector.

Pride of place must go to the first section, "Early Techniques and the Colonial Heritage." Sewing and, as an integral part of it, quilting was "woman's work" from the time of the first European settlements in America. But pre-nineteenth-century quilts are of utmost rarity. Almost all have been destroyed by age and use. A few late-eighteenth-century pieces do remain, but even these are extremely uncommon, perhaps as rare as unremodeled eighteenth-century houses. The very early modes of quiltmaking, however, did continue into the first third of the nineteenth century, and most of them are included here. Of the technical variations, stuffed work is represented by two bedcovers, one dated 1796 (no. 2), and the other 1808 (no. 4). Glazed wool worsted (no. 3), stencil work (no. 5) and crewel work (no. 6) are shown in very fine examples. Amanda's candlewick spread (no. 1) is our "first quilt" mentioned above. It represents the rare embroidery spreads of this period. Finally, Broderie Perse, the cutting out of whole motifs from printed fabrics and stitching of them into a new design on a different background (no. 7 — our example can be dated by its fabrics to c. 1825), was a late Colonial

Details of no. 5.

Detail of no. 8.

Detail of no. 18.

technique that continued into the nineteenth century. Of the early kinds of bedcovers, only needlework bed rugs and coverlets woven by hand or machine are missing. We simply do not consider them quilts, even in the widest possible sense of that often misunderstood term.

The gradual disappearance of these techniques and their replacement by patterns and styles that we recognize easily today are the theme of the second section, "Quilts Come of Age." *Star of Bethlehem* (no. 8), *Sunburst* (no. 10), *Mariner's Compass* (no. 11), *Princess Feather* (no. 17) and *Feathered Star* (no. 19) are patterns as popular with the traditional quiltmakers of today as they were with the makers of these pre–Civil War examples. The range of this forty-year period goes from the prized album (no. 14), and a similarly elegant *Pineapple* (no. 16), to a "folksy" sampler quilt (no. 12). Several pieces in this group feature the wonderful variety of printed cottons available in that period, and there are two excellent examples of crib quilts (nos. 10 and 15). The prize of this section, in addition to the album quilt, is an appliquéd summer spread showing thirty-six naturalistic leaves on a plain white background (no. 18). It is a stunner!

Detail of no. 14.

Later in the century, in the period covered by the third section, many American quilters were tempted to stray from their earlier traditions, developing the lush trivialities of the Victorian silk quilt (no. 33). The silk taffetas and satins of the crazies were also used for fancy quilts in more conventional patterns (nos. 32 and 34). This high-style Victoriana was, nonetheless, paralleled by a wave of Americana, more agreeable to our eyes today. The Centennial and the 1876 exposition in Philadelphia may account for the usage of our flag's colors in the *Whig's Defeat* variant (no. 22). This accent on patriotism underscores the fact that Pennsylvania continued to be a major center of production for quilts. (Numbers 20–24, 26 and 28 in the third section are known to come from there. Others may also.) Older traditional patterns continued to be used again and again: *Princess Feather* (no. 20), *Log Cabin–Barn Raising* (no. 23), *Basket* (no. 28), *Schoolhouse* (no. 29) and *Triple Irish Chain* in a particularly lovely example (no. 30). The prize of this section is a Royal Hawaiian Flag quilt (no. 27).

The last chronological section has been devoted to certain key movements by quiltmakers in the twentieth century, albeit with some variations. The brilliant quilts of the Amish and Mennonites in both Pennsylvania and Ohio are featured (nos. 35–37 and 39). But along with them is a later Victorian-influenced fancy quilt, *Tumbling Blocks* (no. 34). Not included here are examples of "Depression quilts," to which neither of us feels drawn. Also absent (with two exceptions) are the fascinating productions of contemporary quiltmakers. We have chosen to concentrate here on the antique quilts now, before they become totally unavailable or prohibitively expensive. Perhaps in time our collecting interest will shift to embrace the exciting contemporary movement in quilting.

In the "Collectors' Choice" section is a new blue-and-white quilt specially prepared for this exhibition by my daughter. As she produced *With Hearts and Hands—Homage to Amanda* (no. 1b) as a token of respect to her great-great-great-grandmother, so she prepared *Coastal Waters* (no. 47) as a celebration of the quilter's heritage and as a coda to the exhibition itself.

Edwin Binney, 3rd

HOMAGE TO AMANDA

Early Techniques and the Colonial Heritage

*C*andlewicking is an embroidery technique in which a design is worked on the foundation cloth, in densely spaced, looped stitches kept uniform in length by the use of a reed or some similar gauge. Upon completion, the loops are cut, and the spread is hot-washed to tighten the foundation cloth and compact its embroidered pile. (The chenille bedspreads of the mid–twentieth century are the machine-produced equivalents of these early American bedcovers.)

Although most early candlewick spreads emphasize outline motifs of sinuous lines of pile, some employ solid areas, as does this example. This later, nineteenth-century stylistic variation is rather close in feeling to the effects created by stuffed work (see no. 2). Representative of its genre, this spread also possesses fringe. However, the original fringe, which bordered three sides, was greatly damaged. During conservation, it was repaired to provide complete borders for only two sides.

It should be noted that very few American bedcovers in any medium and any period are as completely identified by their makers as has been this example. The elegant flourished embroidery of the signature, place and date are, reasonably, a reflection of the then-eighteen-year-old Amanda's pride (and, perhaps, relief) at the completion of her ambitious and well-executed project.

"Amanda Davisson Shelby Cty Ky June 17 1826". Note the long double "s" which appears in her signature.

Measurements are given as width × length.

1. All-white, Amanda Davisson, Shelby County, Kentucky, 1826, 75 × 87 inches, cotton, tufted embroidered candlewick. See detail for signature and date.

1a. Amanda Davisson Millar (1808-1897). This portrait of her was painted c. 1840-1850.

Amanda Davisson, eldest child of Dr. Andrew W. (1783-1822) and Rebecca Todd Davisson, was born in Lawrenceburg, Indiana, whence her family had moved from Xenia, Ohio. Her father's ancestors had been in America since 1651. James Todd, Rebecca's father, fourth of the name in a family originally Scottish, had arrived from Northern Ireland in 1764. He served in the Revolutionary War. Rebecca's maternal grandfather, John Buchanan, after service in the same war, was killed by Indians in 1791 at the door of the fort (called Buchanan Station) he had built near Nashville, Tennessee.

Rebecca Todd Davisson (1790-1870), Amanda's mother, was remembered by a granddaughter as "sewing for the poor a great deal" and "sitting in her chair reading or sewing all day." Amanda, like every other American woman of the time, learned to sew early. In a narrative left at her death for the daughter with whom she lived for the forty-three years of her widowhood, she mentioned that "I had made and embroidered a dress for myself when I was but eight years old." When she was eighteen she went to live with her uncle James Todd in Shelby County, Kentucky. There, she prepared and stitched the candlewick spread (no. 1) which is the cornerstone of this quilt collection and exhibition.

After two years of teaching school, Amanda married a Presbyterian minister, James Patterson Millar (1792-1854), and moved with him to his parish in South Argyle, New York. Amanda's portrait is believed to have been painted during this time, in the mid-1840's. In it, we see her as very much the mature and conservative rural minister's wife. Her clear and appraising gaze expresses intelligence and firm responsibility, surely useful qualities in a woman of her station. Her dress, while well-tailored, is inexpensive and rather unfashionable. It is reasonable to suppose that she made it herself, as well as her coif of black chiffon and ribbon.

In 1851, Reverend Millar, with his wife and younger children, answered the call to "convert the heathen" and was sent, via the Isthmus of Panama, to Albany, in the Oregon Territory. They followed closely the similar trek of their eldest daughter, who had been sent to open a school in the same Territory. In 1854, Amanda, her husband and youngest daughter Ella, aged six, were passengers on the second trip of the ill-fated steamboat *Gazelle* on the Willamette River near Salem, Oregon. When the boiler exploded, Reverend Millar, who had just gone on deck, was killed instantly. Amanda, in the ladies' saloon, was thrown across the room, covered with debris, her ribs broken. She retained throughout the rest of her life small bits of quicksilver from a shattered mirror which pitted her face. Family reports claim these were not noticeable. After her recovery, Amanda returned to her family in the East. She died in Washington, D.C. in 1897, one year before the birth of Edwin Binney, 3rd's mother, her great-granddaughter.

This quilt is a simple, sentimental "thank you" in cloth to my great-great-great-grandmother Amanda, whose work was a major influence in my choice of quiltmaking as a vocation.

The muted colors in the new fabrics were chosen to blend with the colored scraps from an antique quilt which were used to make the three-dimensional hands. It was important to me to include fragments of cloth from the era in which Amanda lived.

Gail Binney-Winslow

Each generation of a family seems to have one member who is interested in family genealogies more than the others. An older sister of Edwin Binney, 3rd's maternal grandmother was the family member who spent years of her life tracing ancestors and keeping records. It is from the autobiographical notes of each generation of Amanda's female descendants, collected and copied by this great-aunt, that the present account has been prepared.

One of the most time-consuming techniques of the early American quiltmaker's art was stuffed work. Having joined together two layers of cloth by the quilted outlines of the decorative motifs, the stitcher had to open tiny holes in the back of each motif, ideally by parting the threads of the cloth without breaking them. The stuffing was then pulled in with a bodkin through these openings, which were closed by realigning with a needle the threads of the cloth. There was little allowance for false steps; if the quilter wished to remove a motif, it was difficult or impossible to repair the distortion of the cloth caused by the stuffing. A sure eye and a sure hand were the required adjuncts to a vigorous preliminary planning. The free-form nature of the technique, unrestricted by geometric pieced work or dynamic color contrasts, required of the successful quiltmaker a sure sense of design as well.

The theme of the *Flowering Tree* (as it was called by its East Indian originators) was a popular choice for this technique at the turn of the nineteenth century, combining easily recognized shapes with a coherent overall organization. Designs of this type were inspired by imported East Indian *palampores,* hangings or spreads of printed and painted cotton which were highly prized and expensive. This influence can be seen in this quilt's variety of exotic flowers issuing from common branches and, in particular, in the pyramids of balls grouped around the border, a free adaptation of the pyramidal hills in the Indian *palampores.*

2. *All-white, 1796, origin unknown, 87 3/4 × 92 1/4 inches (including fringe), cotton. Techniques include stuffed work and cording. Two-and-one-quarter-inch woven cotton string fringe with each strand knotted (section omitted at top is original). Some twentieth-century repairs in fringe.*

PUBLISHED: *Cyril I. Nelson,* The Quilt Engagement Calendar 1984, *no. 25.*

*I*t has been usual for American quilt enthusiasts to describe almost all early woolen quilts as linsey-woolseys. This homey term, which can be traced in English references back to the sixteenth century, properly refers to a coarse utility fabric combining a linen warp and a wool weft, most suitable for winter hangings and upholstery. Although this fabric was certainly available in America throughout the eighteenth century (it was, for example, imported by the Hudson Bay Company for trade with the Indians), there were many other English woolens available that were far better suited for use in quilts.

Principal among these were the various worsteds manufactured in Norwich, England and similar centers. These were also favored for warm and sturdy hangings and upholstery, and were admired near the end of the eighteenth century for their surprisingly strong, clear colors and large, uncomplicated patterns. Typical also of the Norwich worsteds was the lustrous heavy glazing seen in this example, which was accomplished by calendering the cloth under great weight and heat. (The glazes of later cotton prints, although usually burnished, consist of less firmly applied resin solutions or egg emulsions, and are correspondingly less wear-resistant.)

It would be natural to assume that such a heavy fabric would preclude fine stitchery, but this example is but one proof that such was not the case. The various floral motifs quilted into the individual diamond shapes are painstakingly stitched.

This worsted quilt is particularly rare in that it is pieced of many colors. Most worsted and linsey-woolsey quilts were of one color, finely quilted. Such monochromatic creations were probably the more popular in their day because they could add a sense of formality and magnificence to a bedchamber. The pieced examples were often made from remnants of cloth, saved over time. Yet it is these pieced quilts that have come down to us in very limited numbers, making them the treasured examples today.

Finally, note should be made of the floral duotone damask side panels. This English fabric dates from the last quarter of the eighteenth century, although its pattern originated in mid-century. The panels are pieced of many remnants, underscoring the fact that such material was treasured, none of it wasted.

3. One Patch *variation, attributed to Eunice Farrer Chamberlain, near Plattsburgh, New York, c. 1800, 100 × 102 inches, pieced and glazed wool worsteds.*

PUBLISHED: *Kiracofe and Kile,* The Quilt Digest 2, *page 23.*

The initials and date flank a two-handled neo-classic urn on a platform pedestal, the urn topped by a pineapple finial. Other decorative motifs include ribbon festoons and sprigs of grape, rose, acorn and other plant forms. The urn with floral sprays was a popular convention derived from European neoclassic sources, and has been used well here to disguise the central seam of the cloth necessitated by the narrow loom widths of the period.

Memorial urns, with or without funerary associations, were particularly popular devices in Federal Period America, and examples can be readily found in all of the arts media of the time. The delicacy and balance of the motifs in this example overcome any theorem-like stiffness. Such delicacy and balance are the products of an advanced design talent coupled with an extraordinary needlework ability. Few early All-white spreads, no matter how fine, can match this one for its artistic and technical merit. The quilt is even rarer for its early corded date and initials.

(The fineness of this quilt prevents its inclusion in the extended exhibition tour of this collection, after the initial showing in San Diego.)

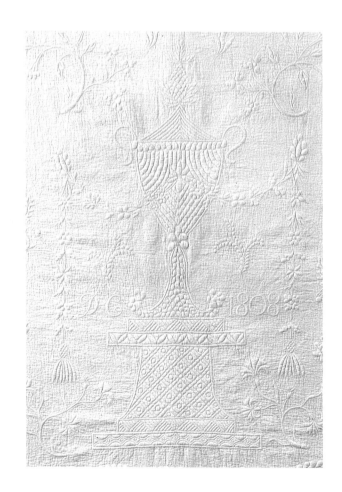

4. All-white, 1808, found in Burlington, Vermont, 93 × 98 inches (including fringe), cotton. Techniques include stuffed work, cording and stipple quilting. Initialed "D C" and dated at the center of the quilt. Three-inch, knotted-netting cotton thread fringe with small tassels, on three sides, with some nineteenth-century wool repairs.

PUBLISHED: Kiracofe and Kile, The Quilt Digest 2, page 4 (detail).

Stenciling was a major technique in the decoration of household articles in America during the early part of the nineteenth century. Furniture and tinware are the most obvious and numerous examples. The homemaker tried her hand at stenciling fabric as well. Spreads such as this example were items of rural home production made especially in New England and New York State, particularly in the 1820's and 1830's. Not many of these attractive textiles have survived; very few are housed in public or private collections.

Close examination of the motifs in this spread (some of which, like the morning glories, are quite rare) reveals that small stencils were used repeatedly to build up finished motifs (much as the Baltimore quiltmaker built up layers of appliqué work in her quilt—see no. 14), a characteristic of relatively early examples of this short-lived technique. The formal arrangement of the motifs corroborates an early date as well. The design, while attractive, is archaic in its conception and choices. It shows a strong affinity with eighteenth-century American embroidered spreads and hangings (see no. 6), as much as it recalls the fashions of the later Federal Period in which it was made.

To make such a spread, the stenciler would cut stencils from heavy paper, stiffened fabric or tin. The process is painstaking and laborious, not to mention time-consuming. The highly concentrated dyes that were used for stenciling were occasionally caustic, and such is the case here. The green used for the leaves has uniformly degraded the cotton fabric to an extent that numerous holes have appeared where leaves once were.

(Despite extensive conservation, the fragility of this rare piece precludes it from travel, after its initial showing in San Diego.)

  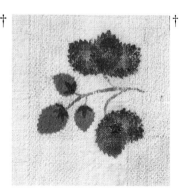

5. Stenciled spread, c. 1810–1830, New England, 92 × 94 inches, cotton. Initialed "E.S" at the top of the spread. Woven tape cotton thread fringe twisted in bundles, on three sides. Floral and fruit motifs include peonies, roses, morning glories, tulips, violas and strawberries.

31

6. Crewel work spread, c. 1810–1830, found in Connecticut, 77 × 93½ inches (including fringe), embroidered wool yarn on cotton.

*A*n old European form of surface decoration, crewel embroidery was not limited in the bedchamber to bedspreads, but was also worked onto matching bed curtains and valances. In English Stuart times, the work was as geometric as the common design books of the period suggest, and was usually rather dark. In the American Colonies, the copybooks, as they were called, were scarce and designs, subsequently, became less controlled. This spread, in a remarkable state of preservation, possesses an open, airy design, reflecting its American heritage. Yet its very existence underscores the influence of English tradition that was shortly to be superseded by American innovations in quilting, appliqué and piece work.

The early crewel work of the Colonies and new nation is somewhat less rare than other techniques. Superb examples exist in several museum collections, and are reproduced in books.

*B*roderie Perse is a technique in which motifs from printed fabrics are cut out and then appliquéd in a new design to a new ground, usually of white cotton. The resulting amalgam frequently surpasses the aesthetic interest of the original printed fabrics, which were usually overall drop repeat glazed chintzes. These repeat motifs, isolated and combined by the quiltmaker in a formal composition, achieve a clarity and visual richness that would be unexpected in their original contexts.

As with many of the techniques illustrated in this first section, Broderie Perse typifies a popular English technique adopted by Colonial American quiltmakers and continued into the Federal Period for uniquely American reasons. One might say that Broderie Perse in England was the textile equivalent of paper découpage, also a popular household pastime. The technique further provides a pleasing pictorial effect that is far less demanding than embroidery, both of the maker's time and artistic skills or confidence. In America, to these factors was added the often-cited scarcity of good printed fabrics. The technique allowed the frugal use of valuable scraps left from other projects, as well as the stretching over a large area of a small piece of expensive cloth. With changes of aesthetics and the increased availability of printed cottons, quilts of this type were made less and less after 1825.

7. Broderie Perse, c. 1825, origin unknown, 61 × 67 ½ inches, appliquéd cottons, pieced cotton borders. Made for a low-post child's bed.

PUBLISHED: Sandi Fox, Small Endearments, *no. 6. Cyril I. Nelson,* The Quilt Engagement Calendar 1981, *no. 41.*

EXHIBITED: Small Endearments: 19th Century Quilts for Children and Dolls *(Los Angeles Municipal Art Gallery, December 9, 1980 ff.).*

Quilts Come of Age

*I*t would be difficult to choose another pieced pattern that typifies the Americanization of quiltmaking more than *Star of Bethlehem*. It is an exuberant design that demands attention, then awe. Early examples such as this one, with their staggering size, are even more prepossessing. By the time this quilt was fashioned, America had established herself as an independent, generally self-sufficient nation. Her people were not affluent, but they were comfortable, and the fabrics employed in America's quilts during this period reflect that ease. This quilt's fabrics are an enviable encyclopedia of the types and styles available to a well-to-do quiltmaker in eastern Pennsylvania.

Technically, the *Star of Bethlehem* is composed of identically-sized diamonds, sewn from a center, each ever-widening row a different color from the preceding row. The piecing requires great accuracy, as the slightest mistake in the inner sections becomes increasingly magnified in succeeding rows. (This construction method is shared with number 10.)

Thus, personal creativity is confined to a standardized form; applications such as the Broderie Perse cut-outs placed between alternate points of this star are incidental to the whole. There is none of the carefree individualism we will see in the third and fourth sections. However, it is obvious that America's quiltmakers are taking charge of their creations. It is also obvious that they intend to be noticed.

8. Star of Bethlehem, *c. 1830–1850, southeastern Pennsylvania, 116 × 116 inches, pieced cottons and appliquéd cotton chintzes.*

9. Variable Star with central medallion motif, c. 1840-1860, eastern United States, 75½ × 91 inches, pieced and appliquéd cottons. Some of the appliqué is padded.

PUBLISHED: *Kiracofe and Kile,* The Quilt Digest 2, *page 25.*

*T*his quilt is visual proof that America's quiltmakers redirected the course of quiltmaking in the nineteenth century. Central medallion quilts, where a centered motif draws the eye, were a classic English form popular during the eighteenth century. Examples made their way to the Colonies and several were made here, repeating the English style. This quilt, too, is of the central medallion style, but how different it is from its earlier English and American cousins. In addition, a central motif is usually large, with narrow borders. Here the opposite is true. Its appliqué and piece work are joined together in one creation, an innovation that carries through to today's contemporary American quilts. And we see an American playfulness in the design motifs selected. This is not a new-world copy of English work; it is truly an American curiosity.

The American child, as the nineteenth century progressed, was idealized in picture and song. Upon reflection, this should not seem surprising in a nation that was young and dependent upon population growth for its survival and expansion. Yet it remains startling to come upon a crib quilt that is as well-designed and finely-crafted as this one. We do not expect that a woman with a large family to rear could spend her time in such a seemingly extravagant fashion, but hundreds of superbly crafted crib quilts from the nineteenth century have been preserved.

From the nineteenth century onward, the crib quilt has been far more than a warm covering for an infant. In a given community of family and friends, women have always made quilts with and for each other, to commemorate personal events like the birth of a child. Crib quilts appropriately celebrate such shared joys, both in examples from the past and in the quilts being made today.

10. Sunburst *crib quilt, c. 1840–1860, origin unknown, 48 × 48 inches, pieced cottons with a woven tape binding.*

PUBLISHED: *Sandi Fox,* Small Endearments, *no. 31. Cyril I. Nelson,* The Quilt Engagement Calendar 1979, *no. 40.*

EXHIBITED: Small Endearments: 19th Century Quilts for Children and Dolls *(Los Angeles Municipal Art Gallery, December 9, 1980 ff.).*

If one were to choose a single characteristic typical of mid-nineteenth-century appliqué quilts, it would be the thorough integration of appliqué designs with adjacent quilting motifs. As any quiltmaker can attest, such integration is so time-consuming that most stitchers allow rationalization to supplant enthusiasm in their work. This quilt possesses such integration. The quilting and stuffed work are not complements to the appliqué patterns; they are equal partners in creating the beauty of this fine work. In this quilt, the viewer will discover many of the decorative motifs so often found in mid-nineteenth-century creations: hearts, acorns, leaves, crescents and stars.

By mid-century, many quiltmakers performed their stuffed work as lap work. Although the particulars might vary, the basic approach was the one employed here. The appliquéd quilt top was marked with quilting guidelines. In each small area to be stuffed, a thin gauze was basted to the back of the quilt top. A running stitch was employed to follow the quilting guidelines, sewing the quilt top to the gauze in each stuffed work area. The area was then stuffed through openings in the gauze (a method similar to that described for number 2). When all these stuffed areas were completed, the basting stitches were removed, and any surplus gauze was trimmed away. A very thin batting and the backing material for the entire top were added, and the piece was quilted. This method can be found in several finely-crafted quilts dating from 1840 to the beginning of the twentieth century.

The quilting between the stuffed work areas is irregular. Some of it is finely done, some less so. This probably indicates that several women performed the quilting, helping the quiltmaker at a bee.

11. Mariner's Compass, *c. 1840–
1860, origin unknown, 77 × 94
inches, pieced and appliquéd cottons, embroidery and stuffed work.*

PUBLISHED: *Cyril I. Nelson,*
The Quilt Engagement Calendar 1982, *no. 45. Cyril I. Nelson
and Carter Houck,* The Quilt Engagement Calendar Treasury, *no.
136.*

12. Sampler, Mrs. Cottrel, Virginia or Kentucky, c. 1850–1870, 75 1/2 × 79 3/4 inches, pieced and appliquéd cottons.

*S*ince the second quarter of the nineteenth century, American quiltmakers have fashioned an innumerable quantity of laudable sampler or album quilts. Two examples of this type of American needlework have been included in this exhibition, one for its sophisticated urban sensitivity (no. 14), and this one for its simple rural charm. It is sometimes difficult for modern viewers, so used to the twentieth-century aesthetic emphasis on a single subject, to judge assembled works of art like album or sampler quilts. When viewing this quilt, we are not looking at a conscious attempt at aesthetic monumentality, but an equally conscious pleasure taken in the creation of an assemblage of favorite motifs. It may be that these separate elements were leftovers from previous quilts, or it may be that this thoughtful quiltmaker assembled in her mind all her favorite patterns before making and joining them into one amalgamation.

The observant viewer will note that quilt patterns for block-style (*North Carolina Lily*) and overall-design quilts (*Irish Chain*) have been incorporated into this work.

*B*y 1850, American quiltmakers were consciously striving to create new styles. A pride in accomplishment, the type that results from growth and expansion, was a hallmark of the era. Americans were forging their own identities. One sees this in the decorative fervor that swept the country. This quilt, with its hearts (to celebrate a wedding?), birds and pineapples, shares surface decorations with other utilitarian household objects of the period such as painted furniture, hooked rugs, frakturs and theorems, which were created by the hundreds of thousands. A style that could be categorized as peculiarly American was evolving. Yet one also sees a residue of the earlier English style, a fussy, decorative expression that complemented its setting rather than imposing itself upon it. It will be another twenty years before we shall see the pre-eminence of vivid, monolithic quiltworks (like no. 26).

13. Unnamed pattern with four hearts, four leaf sprays and four pineapples, c. 1850-1870, Pennsylvania or New York, 89 × 88 ½ inches, appliquéd cottons.

With the possible exception of Amish works, no other type of American quilt has received the attention and adulation afforded the Baltimore Albums. Truly, this small body of needlework stands as a testament to the powers of America's quiltmakers. Add to their technical brilliance the fact that these quilts were fashioned in a specific geographic area during a short period of time and one has the necessary ingredients for promotion and, subsequently, popular acclaim.

All album quilts are the by-products of shared sentiments: friendship, love, reverence and patriotism, to name the most obvious. What makes the Baltimore variety so very special, however, was the advanced competition among a small group of regional needleworkers. This striving for excellence was endemic in any region where quiltmaking was pursued with vigor (southeastern Pennsylvania is another good example), but in this Maryland city and its environs this fervor was unrivaled. It was no doubt spurred by what we now believe to have been several professional quiltmakers who sold their blocks for inclusion in these testimonials. The technical merit of these works is extremely high. The styles and types have been painstakingly documented in Dena S. Katzenberg's fine *Baltimore Album Quilts*. Those interested in learning more about this particular genre of American quiltmaking are urged to read this text.

Katzenberg has underlined the important focus provided by the star as the center of this quilt. Not all Baltimore Album quilts possess such sure balance of construction. This balance is carried through the entire quilt by the way in which the various floral motifs (baskets, wreaths and bouquets, for example) are arranged. As with many album quilts, this one possesses a block filled with Odd Fellows symbology. The initials "F.L.T" stand for the motto of the I.O.O.F., "Friendship, Love and Truth."

Many viewers believe that the Baltimore Album quilts of the 1840's and 1850's mark the apex of American quiltmaking. Some have even gone so far as to claim an obvious decline in technical and creative merit from that era to the present day. We, as students and collectors of American quilts, do not adhere to this judgment. In fact, we would aver that it is the last half of the nineteenth century in which we see the emergence of a truly artistic, individualistic American style. Yet neither will we deride the laudable achievements represented in the album quilts of the mid-nineteenth century, particularly those of Baltimore.

14. *Album, c. 1854, from the George Washington MacKay Young family, Baltimore, Maryland, 105 ½ × 106 inches, appliquéd cottons. Techniques include trapunto, padding and embroidery.*

PUBLISHED: *Dena S. Katzenberg,* Baltimore Album Quilts, *pages 118–119. Kiracofe and Kile,* The Quilt Digest 2, *page 20.*

EXHIBITED: Baltimore Album Quilts *(The Museum of Fine Arts, Houston, November 18, 1980 ff.) (The Metropolitan Museum of Art, New York, June 30, 1981 ff.) (The Baltimore Museum of Art, December 13, 1981 ff.).*

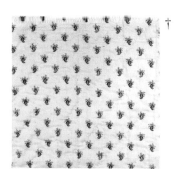

Detail of backing fabric.

15. The Sun *medallion with* Variable Star *crib quilt, c. 1850–1870, found in Ohio, 39¹/₂ × 39¹/₂ inches, pieced cottons.*

PUBLISHED: *Sandi Fox,* Small Endearments, *no. 28.*

EXHIBITED: Small Endearments: 19th Century Quilts for Children and Dolls *(Los Angeles Municipal Art Gallery, December 9, 1980 ff.).*

*A*s with full-sized quilts, most crib quilts were made for daily use. Fine examples such as this one are not typical of the nineteenth century; many crib quilts, for example, were made as learning tools.

This example, like number 10, matches its larger cousins in this exhibition for precision of design and craft. It is also an excellent example of miniaturization, a trait shared by many finer crib quilts from this period. The care and patience taken to cut smaller, more delicate pieces for a crib quilt should not be underestimated. How much simpler it would have been for this quiltmaker if she had used larger pieces left over from making a full-sized quilt. But she, like many of her peers, chose to specially cut and piece smaller fragments into a truly miniature creation.

*I*t is said that American sea captains, returning from the tropics, brought back exotic fruits, among them pineapples. They impaled them on their gate and fence posts to herald their return from the sea. Whether this is folklore or fact, the pineapple has served as a symbol of hospitality and goodwill in Western culture for centuries. America's leading cabinetmakers utilized the pineapple as finial and bas-relief decorations, and needleworkers incorporated the motif into their creations. In this rendition, the quiltmaker has left nothing to conjecture regarding her intent.

16. Pineapple, c. *1860–1880, Pennsylvania, 104 ½ × 104 ½ inches, appliquéd cottons and pieced cotton sashing.*

PUBLISHED: *Robert Bishop,* et al., Quilts, Coverlets, Rugs & Samplers, *no. 190. Cyril I. Nelson,* The Quilt Engagement Calendar 1978, *no. 56.*

*B*y 1850, fabric production in the United States was growing rapidly; however, much of the cloth used by Americans was still made abroad. It is important to note that, during the eighteenth and most of the nineteenth centuries, American trade in foreign textiles was of an economic importance similar to trade in steel or oil today. Some of the fabrics in this quilt, as well as materials seen in many of the pre-Civil War quilts in this exhibition (for example, nos. 3, 7, 8, 10, 11 and 14), are European in origin.

Princess Feather is a pattern one sees in quilts from every region of the country, in every era after 1850. Its graceful yet dynamic style seemed to captivate American quiltmakers. Here it is accented by *Laurel Leaves,* another graceful, though less popular, pattern. This unusual combination is further enhanced by smaller, single feathers in an outer border of great style and merit.

In the center of the feather cluster is the imprint of an ink-stamp with the name of Margaret Boon. Her name has caused previous owners and dealers to try to suggest a relationship to Daniel Boone. Such supposition is not of any real importance. Margaret was too good a needlewoman to need any genealogical support for her artistry. Only those quiltmakers who were secure in their expertise would dare to use such a stamp to mark their work. Margaret Boon knew her own worth then, as we recognize it today.

†

17. Princess Feather *with* Laurel Leaves, *Margaret Boon, Lancaster County, Pennsylvania, c. 1840–1860, 94 × 96 inches, appliquéd and pieced cottons.*

18. Leaves *summer spread, c. 1850–1870, New England, 95×95 inches, appliquéd cotton with padded stems and vine.*

PUBLISHED: *Kiracofe and Kile, The Quilt Digest 1, page 48 (and cover).*

*P*atsy and Myron Orlofsky, in their pioneering text *Quilts in America,* make note of the wealth of plant and flower forms found in America's quilts. No period was richer in their abundance than the middle of the nineteenth century. Rarest in number among these quilts is the botanical quilt. This example, with its restrained design, is a true study of the tree varieties found in New England.

Technically speaking, this is not a quilt, but a summer spread (a quilt top with a finished binding). Yet the time required to draw and cut the thirty-six leaf patterns, added to the industry required to cut the material and appliqué it delicately to the white cotton ground cloth, is awe-inspiring. It is no wonder that few of these extraordinary quilts seem to have been made.

This quilt, with its carefully padded stems and vine, demands the viewer's admiration. Few quilts match the indigo-blue-and-white creations shown in our "Collectors' Choice" for their simple, monumental elegance. This quilt does.

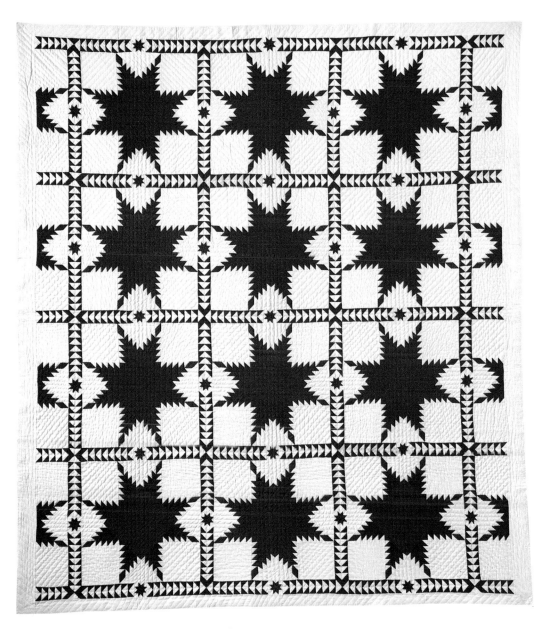

Star patterns appeared on America's quilts from virtually the beginning. No other motif has been represented so profusely. As an example, nine quilts in this section and eighteen works in this exhibition employ stars. Few, however, have so successfully monumentalized the form as this example. The publishers of Safford and Bishop's *America's Quilts and Coverlets* concurred when they chose this quilt to grace their cover.

Fine quilters began experimenting with single colors on white backgrounds earlier in the nineteenth century, but it was at about the time of this quilt's creation that they intensified their efforts. It is a fair assumption that a by-product of their experimentation was the development of variations on existing quilt patterns, and the emergence of new ones. By working in one color on white, a quiltmaker is better able to refine, manipulate and create designs; the distractions inherent in a multitude of printed fabrics or colors are obliterated. The creation of quilts such as this one was a step in the development of the bold geometric patterns we will see in the third and fifth sections.

19. Feathered Star *with* Wild Goose Chase *and* Eight-Pointed Star *sashing, c. 1850–1870, origin unknown, 73 ½ × 80 ½ inches, pieced cottons.*

PUBLISHED: *Carleton L. Safford and Robert Bishop,* America's Quilts and Coverlets, *page 93 (and dust jacket on hardcover volume, cover on paperback volume).*

Americana and Victoriana

Detail of backing fabric.

20. Princess Feather, c. 1875–
1900, Pennsylvania, 88½ × 91½
inches, appliquéd and pieced cottons.

PUBLISHED: Kiracofe and Kile,
The Quilt Digest 2, *page 18.*

*I*t does not take an art critic to see the vast differ-
ence between this quilt and number 17. There is an almost shocking division of
sensitivities displayed in these two works. And yet they are both products of eastern
Pennsylvania. They are, however, approximately forty years removed from each
other, and this quilt is Pennsylvania Dutch. Yet it is the forty years, not genealogy,
that is the dominant factor in their disparity. Color is now arresting; it challenges.
It is this unusual color sense that will continue to be used by Pennsylvania quiltmakers for decades. The design has none of the inner tranquility embodied in
number 17. An entirely new standard has been established, and quiltmakers across
the country follow suit.

Quilt fabric connoisseurs have long admired the beautiful backings chosen by
Pennsylvania quiltmakers. Here is one such example.

Eastern Pennsylvania quiltmakers were among America's most prolific and talented. Among their most time-consuming and cherished creations was a series of variations on *Postage Stamp,* a simple one-patch pattern. The variations carried names, including *Philadelphia Pavement* and *Eye Dazzler.* A variation might take the form of paving stones, set on the diamond, a large central star, or a more complex geometric pattern such as this one.

Quiltmakers are scavengers; they will go to great lengths to secure particular fabrics they desire. This quiltmaker's creation stands as testimony to this fact. Her scrapbag was obviously richly endowed, and she probably purchased fabrics specifically for the construction of this remarkable quilt; her rigorous preparatory planning would have required both.

The patience of any quiltmaker who prepares ten thousand patches of identical size, sews them by hand to each other, and has them come out right, is unrivaled. It takes long enough to count the one hundred rows of one hundred patches each. Imagine the time required to stitch them all together.

21. Postage Stamp *variation, c. 1875-1900, Lancaster or Lebanon County, Pennsylvania, 79 × 79 inches, pieced cottons.*

The Centennial in 1876, and the accompanying exposition in Philadelphia, were centerpieces around which Americans focused their creative energies. Painters, both professional and amateur, cabinetmakers and quiltmakers, among many artisans, attentively fashioned patriotic works for the occasions. This quilt, which dates from the period, is one such example. It is a happy, even joyous, creation that echoes the satisfaction most Americans experienced at their country's advancement. American historical events played a role in the naming of quilt patterns during the nineteenth century. *Burgoyne Surrounded, Clay's Choice* and *Whig's Defeat* are three examples.

Mention should be made of the folded patchwork, commonly referred to as "prairie points," which graces the outer edge of this work.

22. Whig's Defeat *variation,*
c. 1880–1890, Pennsylvania, 90 ×
90 inches, appliquéd and pieced
cottons.

PUBLISHED: *Cyril I. Nelson,* The
Quilt Engagement Calendar 1984,
no. 11.

*I*f one quilt pattern were selected to represent nineteenth-century American quiltmaking, *Log Cabin* would be the obvious choice. From 1850 onwards, it was an overwhelmingly favorite pattern. It is a safe assumption that virtually any prolific quiltmaker made at least one version of this quintessential pattern.

The *Log Cabin,* whose individual strips are sewn to resemble the construction of a primitive dwelling, appears in two basic types. One of these features block-style repetitiveness. Examples of this style are variations named *Pineapple, Windmill Blades, Courthouse Steps* and *Light and Dark.* The other type consists of overall patterns, which are best represented by *Straight Furrow* (no. 38) and, as seen here, *Barn Raising.*

All of these variations feature pattern blocks divided into light and dark sections. By manipulating the arrangement of these tonalities, a quiltmaker is able to produce the many pattern variations. The red squares found at the center of each pattern block in this quilt are called "chimneys" or "hearths." They are meant to represent the warm, welcoming fire that was kept going continuously for warmth and cooking. All *Log Cabin* quilts possess "chimneys," although not all are red, or this large (*cf.* no. 32).

The fine array of late-nineteenth-century fabrics utilized in this quilt reads like an encyclopedia of styles and varieties. Most interesting is the printed wool challis, fabric which was held in high esteem by American quiltmakers for its versatility and handling ease.

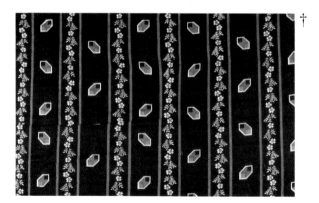

Detail of backing fabric.

23. Log Cabin–Barn Raising, *attributed to a member of the Lentz family, Lebanon County, Pennsylvania, c. 1875–1890, 81 × 81 1/2 inches, wool challis and cottons with a wool twill tape binding.*

PUBLISHED: *Cyril I. Nelson,* The Quilt Engagement Calendar 1981, *no. 12.*

*24. Joseph's Coat, c. 1880–1900,
Pennsylvania, 85 ½ × 80 inches,
pieced cottons.*

*T*he Coat of Many Colors which the doting patri-
arch Jacob gave to his favorite son Joseph and which contributed largely to the boy's
being sold into Egypt by his brothers is mentioned in the Bible (Genesis XXXVII,
verses 3 and 23). Not having an authentic garment for comparison, the nineteenth-
century quiltmaker had free rein.

Quilts with Biblical connotations (see also nos. 8 and 46) were a staple item
throughout nineteenth-century quiltmaking. But this particular pattern, with its
strong diagonal border which creates visual movement, was made almost exclu-
sively in southeastern Pennsylvania, another example of regionalism in American
quilt history.

By the late nineteenth century, American quilt-makers were not only experimenting with pieced geometric patterns, but creating individualistic statements in appliqué as well. Although pictorial appliqué quilts were fashioned earlier in the nineteenth century, perhaps none had the raw, explosive power of this later example. The force of creative change is certainly visible in this quilt.

Although it displays unique creativity, this quilt is not devoid of references to its quiltmaking past. The birds in the border treatment are reminiscent of those in number 13, and the use of leaves and vegetation as major motifs was seen in numbers 11 and 18. However, the inherent reticence seen in earlier quilts has disappeared. Individual flair and creativity are now the standards by which to judge merit.

25. Original design with twenty-one birds in the border, c. 1880–1900, found in Ohio, 68½ × 87½ inches, appliquéd cottons.

PUBLISHED: *Kiracofe and Kile,* The Quilt Digest 2, *page 17.*

*M*ore than any other quilt in this exhibition, this one exemplifies the strong graphic qualities seen in so many late-nineteenth-century pieced creations. Although Pennsylvania quiltmakers more than others utilized bright, solid fabrics to minimize any interference with the geometric power of the pattern, this movement toward creating strong, visual statements was national in scope. Although America's quiltmakers may not have discussed their changing quiltmaking habits as we dissect them today, they were aware of the differences between their quilts and those of their mothers and grandmothers.

Pattern variations like this one, which were the by-products of experimentation with older, established patterns (in this case, the star), went beyond the accepted and established norms of quiltmaking. This is, without question, the American quiltmaker's greatest legacy to her craft. And it is a legacy that we see alive and well today. In no period since the late nineteenth century has the creative push for change been more ardent or successful than in the past ten years in this country. One hundred years from now, the current era may be looked back upon with the same sense of accomplishment as that represented by this remarkable quilt.

26. Carpenter's Wheel, *c. 1880–1890, Lebanon or Lancaster County, Pennsylvania, 84½ × 85½ inches, pieced cottons.*

PUBLISHED: *Cyril I. Nelson,* The Quilt Engagement Calendar 1982, *no. 43.*

*R*ecent research by Hawaiian Elizabeth Akana, published in *The Quilt Digest 3*, finally establishes the place these remarkable quilts hold in American quiltmaking history. Her article, "Ku'u Hae Aloha," is well worth reading. In it, Akana unravels the long, tortured history of these stunning, rare quilts. They appear to date from approximately 1845, and are being made into the present day. Among the earliest examples in existence, however, are those from the late nineteenth century, such as this one. The climate in the Islands contributes to the degradation of all fabrics and, thus, the loss of earlier quilts. Conservation is a problem all quilt enthusiasts must face, but that task is nowhere more immediate than in Hawaii.

The four flags are those of the island kingdom. Each stripe represents a major island; the canton contains a representation of the British Union Jack. The Hawaiian flag reflects an early association between Great Britain and Hawaii.

The mystique of the Royal Hawaiian Flag quilt as a symbol of a vanished island kingdom and as the repository of the *mana,* or spirit, of the quiltmaker accounts for the reticence of present-day Hawaiian owners to publicize their most prized possessions. This also helps explain why so few Royal Hawaiian Flag quilts have emigrated to the Mainland. It is likely that this example will be the only one to have been seen by the vast majority of visitors to this exhibition.

27. *Royal Hawaiian, c. 1880–1900,
Hawaii, $71^{1}/_{2} \times 71^{1}/_{2}$ inches, pieced
and appliquéd cottons. Inscribed:
"Hawaii Ponoi" (Hawaii's Own).*

PUBLISHED: *Cyril I. Nelson,* The
Quilt Engagement Calendar 1982,
*no. 46. Cyril I. Nelson and Carter
Houck,* The Quilt Engagement
Calendar Treasury, *no. 83.*

28. Basket, c. 1880–1900, Pennsylvania, 77 × 77 inches, pieced and appliquéd cottons.

*V*irtually every quiltmaker in the late nineteenth century used cotton prints (or calicoes, as they are commonly called). First imported from England, then manufactured here in enormous quantities and styles, these simple cotton fabrics dictated, through their variety and number, the style and character of America's quilts. These fabrics were available everywhere, even in pioneer America where they were treasured possessions not to be wasted. Catalogues and mail-order houses offered them in abundance, and every dry-goods store stocked them plentifully. It is little wonder, therefore, that Americans with scant knowledge of their quilt heritage often describe calico quilts when asked what they know about this distinct American art; in number alone they are without rival.

Baskets have long been a favorite motif in quilts. We have seen them already in numbers 2, 5–7 and 14. Yet, in these previous examples, the basket was part of a larger motif. Here it has been romanticized in earth-tone calicoes, appearing singly, empty, as a monument to an earlier, less-mechanized past. By the turn of the twentieth century, Americans knew they were no longer a bucolic, agrarian nation, and they rushed to idealize a bygone era.

The *Schoolhouse* is one of the favorite and most easily recognized patterns in the quilter's repertoire. It was popularized in the late nineteenth century and is still made today in great numbers. It has, in effect, proven its longevity. Because the pattern is so common, only the truly individual presentation stands out artistically. This one, created in calicoes, has a homey feeling so prevalent in many of the finest *Schoolhouse* examples.

29. Schoolhouse *in a* Garden Maze, *c. 1890–1910, origin unknown, 92 × 81 inches, pieced cottons.*

PUBLISHED: *Robert Bishop and Patricia Coblentz,* New Discoveries in American Quilts, *page 41.*

*A*n experienced quiltmaker who has created a number of successful quilts consciously makes an important decision at some point: whether to attempt "the perfect quilt." Most choose to meet the challenge, but a very small number have the ability, patience or stamina to achieve what we see here. Simple in pattern, yet monumental in effect, this work stands out above others because it combines striking color choices with flawless technique. It literally glistens.

Brilliant examples such as this one were stored away, brought out into the light of day on special occasions only, and saved for future generations. As a result, a disproportionately large number of exceptionally fine quilts have survived to the present day. Their makers and admirers regarded them as works of art, even though they might not invoke such a phrase to describe them. Hopefully, we will not share in their hesitancy.

The phrase "bride's quilt" is often used to describe these staggering works. Seldom, however, is the quilt in question one that was made to commemorate a marriage. And, although we have no proof that this quilt inscribed "Manda and Glen Binkley" was created to celebrate their union, it is tempting to hope that such was the case.

 †

30. Triple Irish Chain, *1898, northeastern Ohio, 71 × 83 inches, pieced cottons. "Manda and Glen Binkley" and the date are embroidered near the bottom of the quilt.*

PUBLISHED: *Cyril I. Nelson,* The Quilt Engagement Calendar 1982, *no. 51.* Quilts: A Tradition of Variations, *no. 18.*

EXHIBITED: Quilts: A Tradition of Variations *(Mills College Art Gallery, Oakland, California, October 9, 1982 ff.).*

31. New York Beauty *variation,*
c. 1890–1910, origin unknown,
71 1/2 × 74 1/2 inches, pieced cottons.

PUBLISHED: *Cyril I. Nelson,* The
Quilt Engagement Calendar 1975,
no. 22. Carleton L. Safford and
Robert Bishop, America's Quilts
and Coverlets, *page 104.*

*B*y the end of the nineteenth century, needle-
workers had experimented extensively with geometric patterns. With this explora-
tion came a willingness to utilize asymmetry. In the process, the early-nineteenth-
century emphasis upon symmetry ceded its pre-eminence to geometric dynamism.
In this quilt, for example, we see asymmetry coupled with a dramatic pattern;
however, we are impressed by its visual power more than we are disturbed by its
imbalance.

*V*ictorian needleworkers, urged by the numerous women's magazines of the day, created not only *Crazy* quilts in silks, satins and velvets, but other patterns as well. The most often utilized was *Log Cabin*. It doesn't take much imagination to contemplate the tedium brought on by sewing thousands of tiny silk *Log Cabin* strips to a ground cloth.

Although the *Crazy* quilt was highly ornamental, most of the *Log Cabin* quilts produced in these fabrics are austerely controlled. The fans in the four corners of the border reflect the Oriental motifs permeating the decoration of the period. "Gilding the lily," though discreetly at the edges, was still the norm.

32. Log Cabin–Barn Raising variation, c. 1880–1900, origin unknown, 61 × 61 inches, silks.

The Victorian *Crazy* quilt was a passing fad that, for a short time, replaced the ordered quality of geometric pattern with the fussy minutiae of late-nineteenth-century pseudo-elegance. In parlors overfilled with carved gewgaws, stuffed birds under glass bells, antimacassars on chair backs and arms, the *Crazy* quilt at times left the bedroom to become an integral part of salon decoration. Often it was found displayed on a table or over an uncomfortable sofa, where its presence in a place of honor precluded its practical use.

Seldom was it a quilt in any technical sense. Its fussy piecing and supplemental embroidery, the fragility of its silks, satins and velvets, did not lend themselves to true quilting. It was, however, an important innovation as it, even more than friendship quilts where individuals signed their names and messages to pattern blocks, was the quilter's sentimental diary. It might include fabrics and memorabilia from neighbors or absent family members, and private messages known only to the maker. Although its style seems alien to pieced calico quilts of the late nineteenth century, many American needleworkers fashioned a *Crazy*.

For collectors who admire overall patterns, graphically arranged on simple backgrounds, the *Crazy* frequently seems a horrifying aberration. But this example presents a typical *Crazy* border of excellent facture surrounding a field with a more ordered pattern.

33. Hexagonal Star *with* Crazy
border, *c. 1880–1900, found in
Nantucket, Massachusetts, 51 ½ ×
51 ½ inches, pieced, appliquéd and
embroidered silks and velvets.*

The Turn of the Century and Thereafter

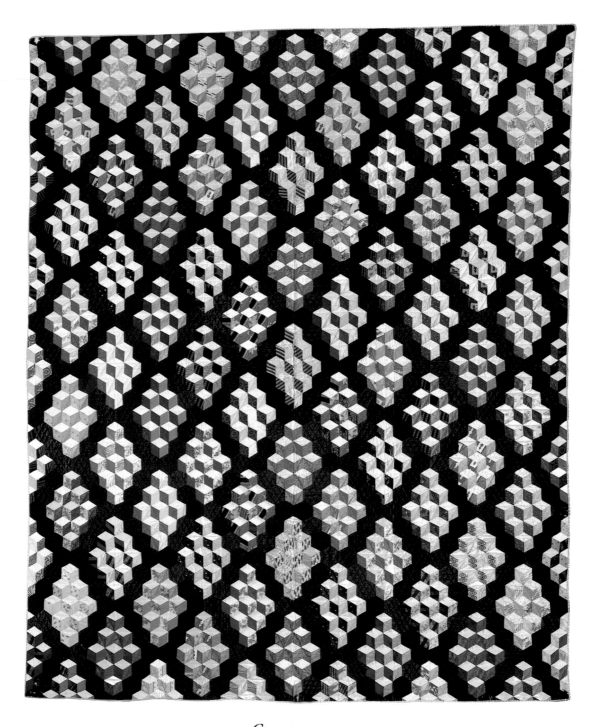

34. Tumbling Blocks *variation, c. 1875–1900, origin unknown, 75¹/₂ × 90¹/₂ inches, pieced silks and velvets.*

PUBLISHED: *Kiracofe and Kile, The Quilt Digest 2, page 19.*

*C*lose behind *Crazy* and *Log Cabin* quilts in the lexicon of silk works is *Tumbling Blocks*. This extraordinary pattern, with its three-dimensional emphasis, would be effective in any fabric as long as the quiltmaker understood that shading and color are its all-important characteristics. Yet, in patterned silks, *Tumbling Blocks* possesses added depth and dynamic. Such *Tumbling Blocks* quilts, though rooted in the Victorian era, were made well into the early twentieth century, as were other silk works, including *Crazy* quilts. It is worthy of note that the architectural use of positive and negative space to create an illusion, as here, is the basis of many of today's contemporary quilts.

*S*olid-fabric Mennonite quilts, like their Amish cousins, tend toward visual purity of form, and many have a kinetic quality. Few, however, have an added dimensionality to match this quilt. Its designer achieved three-dimensional layering by sewing the cloth with a folded, rather than a pressed, seam. Cursory inspection suggests a certain restraint. Closer study reveals a visual energy created by the vivid color contrast, the three-dimensional construction and the jagged *Sawtooth* border.

35. Log Cabin variation, c. 1890–1910, Pennsylvania Mennonite, 71 1/2 × 71 1/2 inches, wool with black silk binding. "Florence Bachstad" is embroidered in red silk thread on a white cotton label which is pinned to the backing.

36. Sawtooth Diamond, 1918,
Lancaster County (Pennsylvania)
Amish, 74 × 75 inches, pieced wools.
Initialed "M. S." and dated in the
quilting just above the binding
at the midpoint in two opposite
borders.

The creations of Amish quilters are among the most prized by modern-day collectors, and sometimes overpraised. This is not surprising. Their forms and coloring mirror, in many aspects, the minimalism of modern painting and printmaking. In virtually all finely-crafted Amish quilts, however, there is an abundance of quilted motifs to soften the stark geometry of the pieced patterns. In this example, calla lilies are utilized for this purpose.

Among the most simply patterned, yet visually dynamic, of Amish quilts are those from Lancaster County, Pennsylvania. *Sawtooth Diamond,* an often-repeated Lancaster design, aptly demonstrates this simplicity. Such statements, however, were not restricted to Pennsylvania (see no. 39).

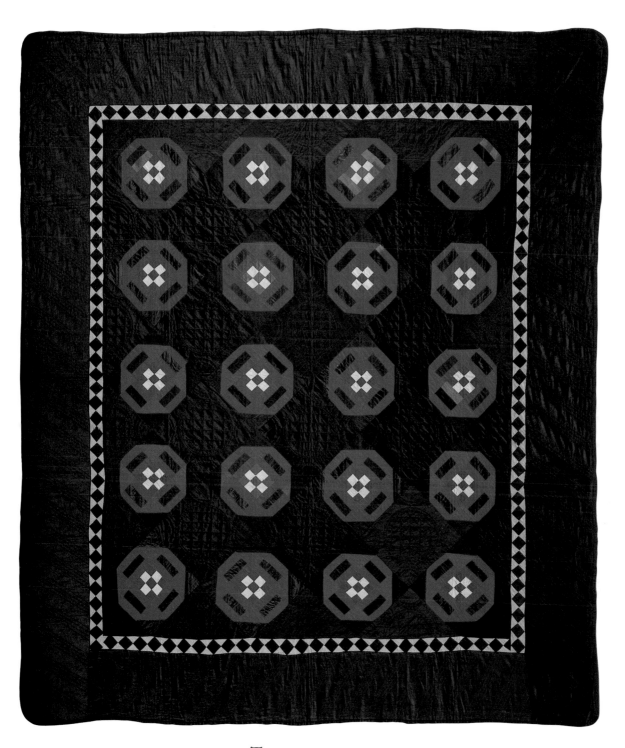

·*T*he Amish of Ohio, Indiana and the later communities of Illinois, Kansas and Iowa incorporated far more complex patterns into their quiltmaking repertoires than the earlier Pennsylvania settlements. Elaborate designs based upon *Nine Patch* and *Four Patch* constructions are typical of this movement towards diversity. This is one such example.

During the first quarter of the twentieth century, the Ohio Amish incorporated cotton sateens into their quilts. This lustrous fabric added dimension to the visual nature of their creations. Here a black cotton sateen is used to great purpose.

37. Burnham Square *with* Nine Patch *center, c. 1920–1940, Ohio Amish, 71 × 84 inches, pieced cotton sateen and cottons.*

Detail of backing fabric.

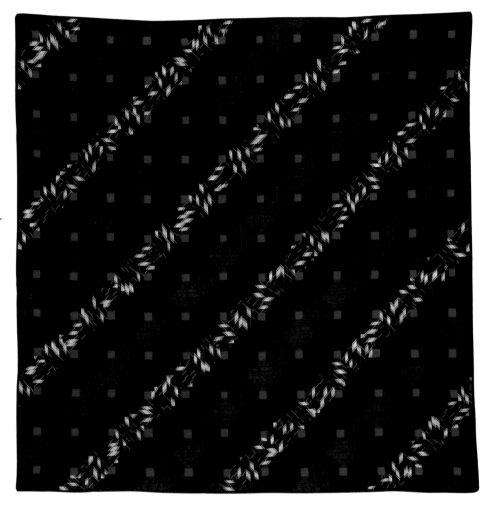

38. Log Cabin–Straight Furrow,
*c. 1910–1930, Pennsylvania, 70¹/₂ ×
70 inches, wools and artificial silk.*

PUBLISHED: *Cyril I. Nelson,* The
Quilt Engagement Calendar 1981,
no. 15.

*A*s has been seen in the quilts presented here,
America's needleworkers constantly recycled patterns. In this example, the familiar
Log Cabin variation called *Straight Furrow* is enlivened by a twentieth-century
quiltmaker. Such refinement and execution of established patterns remain a hallmark of many of today's quiltmakers. Although much experimentation is occurring
with original designs, many are maintaining particularly close links to their quiltmaking heritage by focusing their attentions on traditional patterns and techniques.

The Amish penchant for fine quilting cannot be better illustrated than in this simple but dramatic work. Great stress was placed upon choosing elaborate quilting designs, and much time was taken to decorate the less ornamental, starkly-pieced patterns with finely-wrought quilting.

39. Double Inside Border, c. 1920–1940, Ohio Amish, 80 × 63½ inches, pieced cotton sateens.

PUBLISHED: *Kiracofe and Kile, The Quilt Digest 2, page 22.*

Collectors' Choice

40. Unnamed pattern, c. 1850–1870, New York, 82 1/2 × 99 inches, appliquéd cottons. Initialed "J. F." in embroidery on the backing.

*C*ontrary to the norm for indigo-blue-and-white quilts, this example is appliquéd rather than pieced. Unusual also is the predominance of blue over white. As will be seen in the quilts to follow, large white expanses filled with elaborate quilting were favored by quiltmakers working in this genre. But this quilt is earlier than most blue-and-white creations (it dates from approximately the Civil War) and, although such striking creations were made prior to 1850, most were worked during the last quarter of the nineteenth century.

Mention has been made of the competition among quiltmakers, and consequent displays of expertise. This competitive spirit should not be maligned or dismissed. It was, and still is, a healthy component in the development of this art form. During the second half of the nineteenth century, blue-and-white quilts, for reasons yet uncertain, attained status among expert quiltmakers, or those aspiring to high standards. They became the repositories of fine stitchery, and it is within their borders that we see virtuoso quilting.

41. Feathered Star, c. 1860–1880, found in New Jersey, 79¾ × 82¼ inches, pieced cottons.

We have already seen (in no. 22) that a wave of patriotism swept the country at the time of the Centennial celebration. Few quilts could better illustrate this fact than the one shown here. The eagle has been used as a motif in American decorative arts since the Federal Period and appeared profusely on every imaginable type of souvenir during the late nineteenth century.

The eagle repeat motif and the overall design concept of this quilt make it reminiscent of Centennial and earlier Jacquard woven coverlets. Especially during the second quarter of the nineteenth century, these professionally woven coverlets were frequently the best designed and most elaborately patterned textiles seen in the middle-class and rural homes of the Northeast. It seems natural, then, to suppose that these Jacquards would have inspired quiltmakers, who were making textiles of the same scale and function.

42. Rising Sun *(or* Sunflower*)*
with Eagle *border, c. 1870–1880,*
probably Irontown, Michigan,
72¹/₂ × 99 inches, pieced and appli-
quéd cottons. "Nancy Ganong" is
written in ink on a cloth tag sewn
to the backing. According to A
History of the Descendants of
Jean Guenon of Flushing, Long
Island, *published in 1906, Nancy*
Viola Ganong was born in 1852
in Irontown, Michigan.

43. Carpenter's Square, c. 1880–
1900, found in Ohio, 79 × 79
inches, pieced cottons.

PUBLISHED: Kiracofe and Kile,
The Quilt Digest 2, page 24.

*R*emarkable for its graphic power, strangely, this
pattern is rarely seen. When it does appear, renditions are often in blue and white.
This is not surprising; coupled with the simple, geometric strength of the pattern
are large expanses of white in which elaborate quilting can be worked.

*T*his quilt exemplifies the late-nineteenth-century quiltmaker's ability to produce complex patterns. The longer one stares at this quilt, the more complex and interwoven its many geometric shapes become. Note, however, that much of its strength derives from the fact that it is worked in the simple but stately blue-and-white tradition.

44. Sailboat, c. 1880–1900, origin unknown, 67×80 inches, pieced cottons. Initialed "J M D" in red thread on the front.

PUBLISHED: *Jonathan Holstein,* The Pieced Quilt, *page 52. Patsy and Myron Orlofsky,* Quilts in America, *page 264.*

45. Delectable Mountains,
c. 1880–1900, Pennsylvania, 89 ×
91 inches, pieced cottons.

*I*n John Bunyan's *The Pilgrim's Progress,* the De-
lectable Mountains symbolize an edenic hideaway. As with so many of the finest
quilts, this *Delectable Mountains* transcends its ordinary construction : although most
indigo-blue-and-white quilts were made from, at most, three calicoes and a white
background, this example possesses a wide variety of these treasured fabrics. The
attained monumentality is nowhere better observed than in the border, where the
quiltmaker alternated, in and out, the peaks of the mountains. The result suggests
an almost geologic finality.

This quilt pattern has several different names, such as *Tree Everlasting* and *Prickly Path*. We prefer the present title: a quilt of this excellence merits an important designation. *Path of Thorns* recalls the progress of Jesus to Calvary, carrying the cross, wearing the crown of thorns. Biblical titles like *Joseph's Coat* (no. 24) or *Star of Bethlehem* (no. 8) were as common for quilts as were events in American history.

The sharp, simple shape is perfectly suited to work in the blue-and-white medium. Here, the quiltmaker has used a solid blue-black material, heightening the contrast between it and the white alternating pattern. Finely-wrought quilting embellishes the surface.

46. Path of Thorns, c. 1880–1900, origin unknown, 75 × 75 ³/₄ inches, pieced cottons.

Dedicated to the people of Cape Cod. To those who were born here and know no other place, and to those who have chosen it as home above all other places, and to past generations of east-coast quilters who have also produced blue-and-white quilts reflecting their love and ties to coastal waters.

*J*ust as my great-great-great-grandmother Amanda's quilt was the inspiration for my becoming a quilter and collector, my own collecting activity has given rise to many thoughts about my work and creativity. Neither a strict traditionalist, nor involved solely in contemporary design styles, I find myself with one foot planted in each camp, happiest when combining the two.

Quilts throughout our collection reveal the personal histories of the quiltmakers themselves, reflected in their choice of designs and patterns, their use of color and fabric, embodying traditions and technologies of their own time. It is also evident that geography, social and economic circumstances, age and skill play an important part in the execution of each quilt.

In presenting *Coastal Waters* to the collection, I too am revealing a piece of my own personal history. The blue-and-white quilts of the collection are the true meeting ground between my father and me. I have tried to satisfy his passion for bold graphic statements in this quilt. Loving the techniques of both appliqué and piece work, I have combined the two in the design of this quilt. The free form of the appliquéd central medallion represents the flow of my life, and the repetitive piecing of the compass blocks is not just the symbol of New England seafarers but also the geographical points of the compass at which I have lived. The range of blue represents the changing moods of the water surrounding me, as well as my own changing moods.

Handwork is the literal continuing thread of my life. It has always nourished and soothed my soul and been my constant companion in an ever-changing life. In this, I share a very common bond with all women who have ever held a needle. The appliqué, block piecing and quilting are done by hand with great pleasure. The borders pieced by machine are not just a concession to time, but a confession that my stitches are not as strong as those of my machine.

My hope is that the fabrics themselves reveal what is available and in use by quilters today, including fabric designed by Jinny Beyer and a Liberty print brought from England by my mother. For the backing, I chose printed fabric in the tradition of Pennsylvania quilters of the past whom I so admire and with whom I share a common taste in prints and colors.

The present limitations of my skills have often been frustrating, but a quilter with no room for improvement has little to look forward to, no new horizons to conquer.

The commitment of time, labor and love on my part is just one of many such commitments made by quilters today to carry on a treasured tradition of messages in fabric, stitched in memory of those who have come before and for those yet to come.

Gail Binney-Winslow
South Orleans, Massachusetts
March, 1984

47. Coastal Waters, *Gail Binney-Winslow, South Orleans, Massachusetts, 1984, 84×84 inches, pieced and appliquéd cottons.*

Lenice Ingram BACON, *American Patchwork Quilts* (New York, William Morrow & Company, 1973).

Robert BISHOP and Patricia COBLENTZ, *New Discoveries in American Quilts* (New York, E. P. Dutton & Company, Inc., 1975).

Robert BISHOP, William SECORD and Judith Reiter WEISSMAN, *Quilts, Coverlets, Rugs & Samplers* (New York, Alfred A. Knopf, 1982).

William Rush DUNTON, Jr., M.D., *Old Quilts* (Catonsville, Maryland, 1946).

Sandi FOX, *Small Endearments: 19th Century Quilts for Children and Dolls* (Los Angeles, The Los Angeles Municipal Art Gallery Associates, 1980).

Beth and Jeffrey GUTCHEON, *The Quilt Design Workbook* (New York, Rawson Associates Publishers, Inc., 1976).

Carrie A. HALL and Rose G. KRETSINGER, *The Romance of the Patchwork Quilt in America* (New York, Bonanza Books, 1935).

Jonathan HOLSTEIN, *The Pieced Quilt: An American Design Tradition* (New York, Galahad Books, 1973).

Stella M. JONES, *Hawaiian Quilts,* revised edition (Honolulu, The Honolulu Academy of Arts, *et al.,* 1973).

Dena S. KATZENBERG, *Baltimore Album Quilts* (Baltimore, The Baltimore Museum of Art, 1981).

KIRACOFE and KILE (editors), *The Quilt Digest* (San Francisco, Kiracofe and Kile) (1, 1983; 2, 1984).

Penny McMORRIS, *Crazy Quilts* (New York, E. P. Dutton, Inc., 1984).

Cyril I. NELSON (editor), *The Quilt Engagement Calendar* (New York, E. P. Dutton, Inc., 1975 ff.).

Cyril I. NELSON and Carter HOUCK, *The Quilt Engagement Calendar Treasury* (New York, E. P. Dutton, Inc., 1982).

Patsy and Myron ORLOFSKY, *Quilts in America* (New York, McGraw-Hill Book Company, 1974).

      Quilts: A Tradition of Variations (East Bay Heritage Quilters exhibition catalogue, Mills College Art Gallery, Oakland, California, 1982).

Carleton L. SAFFORD and Robert BISHOP, *America's Quilts and Coverlets* (New York, E. P. Dutton & Company, Inc., 1972).

Printed in Hong Kong through Palace Press
Color Separations by Nissha Printing Company, Ltd., Kyoto, Japan.
Typographical composition in Granjon.
Book design by Jeanne Jambu/Kajun Graphics, San Francisco.
Editing assistance by Harold Nadel, San Francisco.
Photographs by Sharon Risedorph and Lynn Kellner, San Francisco.
Photographs marked with † by William S. Chandler, San Diego.